AMID BEAUTIFUL
LANDSCAPES
───────────────
山水间

编写：北京语言大学对外汉语教材研发中心
绘画：袁丽莉

Compiled by Research and Development Center of TCFL Textbooks
Paintings by Yuan Lili

BEIJING LANGUAGE AND CULTURE
UNIVERSITY PRESS

山水间

AMID BEAUTIFUL LANDSCAPES

读诗赏画学汉语
Chinese Poetry and Painting

编写说明
Preface

《山水间——读诗赏画学汉语》是一本介绍中国古典诗歌、展示中国山水画的文化读物，适用对象是具有初中级水平的汉语学习者及对中国古典诗歌、中国山水画感兴趣的外国人。

中国古典诗歌、书法、绘画都是中国传统文化的重要组成部分，中国古人也常有以诗作画、画中题诗的习惯，可谓"诗画不分家"。中国古典诗歌讲究借助客观事物与景物（即意象）塑造意境，抒发情感，而中国山水画同样追求情景相生，二者有"异曲同工"之妙。因此，很多中国古诗、山水画都同时兼有"诗中有画、画中有诗"的特点。将中国古诗用水墨画的形式进行再创造，这两种完全不同的艺术形式的结合，呈现给读者的是视觉和心灵的双重的艺术效果。

本书充分利用古诗与山水画相辅相成的特点，将中国古诗与山水画完美结合。每首古诗配以一幅山水画，学习者既可通过读诗来赏画，亦可通过赏画来学诗。诗画相融，必会使学习事半功倍，快速提升学习者对中国古典诗歌及中国山水画的了解和鉴赏水平。

本书山水画部分由旅居德国的中国传统水墨画画家袁丽莉女士创作。袁女士毕业于上海复旦大学，自幼受家庭熏陶学习国画技艺。1992年随夫携女旅居德国。她凭借天生的艺术才气和对水墨画的执著热爱，经过长期自学苦练，在西方的文化环境中，孕育出了东方的艺术成果。在德国，她既从事绘画教学，又参加各种艺术展览，包括国际艺术展和中国国内的大型展览。其间曾多次获得中国书画大赛奖项。教学方面，慕名到她的画室学习的学生遍及德国许多大中城市。本书中的山水画，正是她绘画艺术成果的集中体现。

本书从浩如烟海的中国古典诗歌中精选30首最著名、最脍炙人口的佳作。这些诗歌创作时间跨度大、内容涵盖广，体裁丰富，有五言诗，有七言诗；有律诗，有绝句；有唐诗，有宋词，各具特色。

本书突出诵读在诗歌学习中的作用，为每首诗标注了汉语拼音，学习者可根据教师指导反复诵读，亦可根据书中所附录音CD，自行模仿学习。考虑到学习者的汉语水平和学习难度，所有的词语注释、诗歌大意均采用英文形式，不作相应扩展，以理解诗歌为主。

希望本书能够给汉语学习者及山水画爱好者带来一丝快慰。

编者
2011年9月

"Amid Beautiful Landscapes—Chinese Poetry and Painting" is a cultural reader introducing classical Chinese poetry and Chinese landscape painting. It is designed for learners of Chinese language at the elementary or intermediate level and foreigners who are interested in classical Chinese poetry and Chinese landscape painting.

Classical Chinese poetry, calligraphy and painting are all important parts of traditional Chinese culture. Ancient Chinese used to depict landscapes in poems and wrote poems in paintings. For them, poetry and painting were inseparable. In classical Chinese poems, feelings are often expressed through the images based on natural objects and sceneries. Similarly, Chinese landscape paintings also integrate feelings with sceneries, though in a different manner. Therefore, ancient Chinese poems often show picturesque characteristics, while landscape paintings are often poetic. When ancient Chinese poems are reproduced in the form of ink-and-wash paintings, the integration of these two different artistic forms has achieved an artistic effect both visually attractive and mentally appealing.

Fully aware that ancient poetry and landscape painting are closely interrelated, this book combines the two into a perfect whole. Each poem in this book is illustrated with a landscape painting so that readers can enjoy the picture through the poem and learn the poem by the aid of the picture. The integration of poetry and painting is sure to facilitate one's learning and quickly enhance one's ability to understand and appreciate classical Chinese poetry and landscape painting.

The artist of the landscape paintings in this book is Ms. Yuan Lili, a Chinese ink-and-wash painter living in Germany. Ms. Yuan is a graduate from Fudan University in Shanghai, who began to learn traditional Chinese painting at an early age under family influence. In 1992, she moved to Germany together with her husband and daughter. With her artistic talent and ardent love for ink-and-wash painting, she has created many works of Oriental-style in the Occidental cultural context after a long time of self-teaching and practice. In Germany, she is a painting teacher as well as a frequent exhibitor in many international and German art exhibitions. She has won several awards in Chinese calligraphy and painting competitions. As a teacher, she has her own studio, which is filled with students from many large or medium-sized cities in Germany. The landscape paintings in this book are an epitome of her achievements in the field of painting art.

Of the numerous classical Chinese poems, the 30 ones in this book are among the most famous and popular. They were created in different times, covering a wide range of themes and styles. There are poems which have five characters in each line and poems which have seven characters. There are octaves, sestets and quatrains. There are Tang poems, Song poems as well as poems from other dynasties.

This book emphasizes the importance of reading aloud in poetry learning. Each poem is provided with Chinese pinyin so that learners can repeat reading it under the teacher's instruction or read it following the CD recording attached to the book. To balance the difficulty with learners' levels of Chinese proficiency, all the poems are simply annotated and paraphrased in English without being further expanded so that readers can focus on learning their meanings.

Wish all of you, no matter Chinese language learners or landscape painting fans, a pleasant journey of reading this book!

The editorial team
September, 2011

目 录

一	梅花‖王安石	3
二	寻隐者不遇‖贾岛	5
三	登鹳雀楼‖王之涣	7
四	鹿柴‖王维	9
五	独坐敬亭山‖李白	11
六	乐游原‖李商隐	13
七	逢雪宿芙蓉山主人‖刘长卿	15
八	江雪‖柳宗元	17
九	宿建德江‖孟浩然	19
十	登幽州台歌‖陈子昂	21
十一	咏柳‖贺知章	23
十二	清明‖杜牧	25
十三	九月九日忆山东兄弟‖王维	27
十四	望庐山瀑布‖李白	29
十五	黄鹤楼送孟浩然之广陵‖李白	31
十六	早发白帝城‖李白	33
十七	绝句‖杜甫	35
十八	题西林壁‖苏轼	37
十九	饮湖上，初晴后雨‖苏轼	39
二十	登飞来峰‖王安石	41
二十一	秋词‖刘禹锡	43
二十二	滁州西涧‖韦应物	45
二十三	游子吟‖孟郊	47
二十四	山居秋暝‖王维	49
二十五	赋得古原草送别‖白居易	51
二十六	送杜少府之任蜀州‖王勃	53
二十七	无题‖李商隐	55
二十八	明日歌‖文嘉	57
二十九	水调歌头（明月几时有）‖苏轼	59
三十	虞美人‖李煜	61

CONTENTS

1	"The Plum Blossom" by Wang Anshi	3
2	"Searching for the Hermit in Vain" by Jia Dao	5
3	"Ascending the Stork Tower" by Wang Zhihuan	7
4	"At the Luzhai Hermitage" by Wang Wei	9
5	"Sitting Alone at Mount Jingting" by Li Bai	11
6	"The Happy Uplands" by Li Shangyin	13
7	"Lodging in the Hibiscus Mountain on a Snowy Night" by Liu Changqing	15
8	"Snow on the River" by Liu Zongyuan	17
9	"Night Spent on the Jiande River" by Meng Haoran	19
10	"On the Top of Youzhou Tower" by Chen Zi'ang	21
11	"Ode to the Willow" by He Zhizhang	23
12	"On the Qingming Day" by Du Mu	25
13	"Thinking of My Brothers at Home on the Double Ninth Festival" by Wang Wei	27
14	"A View of the Waterfall at Lushan Mountain" by Li Bai	29
15	"Seeing Meng Haoran Off to Guangling at the Yellow Crane Tower" by Li Bai	31
16	"Departure at Morn from Baidi Town" by Li Bai	33
17	"A Quatrain" by Du Fu	35
18	"Written on the Wall of Xilin Temple" by Su Shi	37
19	"Drinking on the West Lake, Enjoying the Rain after the Sunshine" by Su Shi	39
20	"Ascending Feilai Peak" by Wang Anshi	41
21	"Autumn Song" by Liu Yuxi	43
22	"The West Ravine in Chuzhou" by Wei Yingwu	45
23	"Song of a Wanderer" by Meng Jiao	47
24	"An Autumn Evening in the Mountains" by Wang Wei	49
25	"Grass on the Ancient Plain—Farewell to a Friend" by Bai Juyi	51
26	"Farewell to Prefect Du on His Way to Shuzhou" by Wang Bo	53
27	"No Title" by Li Shangyin	55
28	"Song of Tomorrow" by Wen Jia	57
29	"When Did the Moon Become Clear and Bright" by Su Shi	59
30	"To the Tune of 'Fair Lady Yu'" by Li Yu	61

山水画一

Painting No. 1

1 梅花

宋·王安石

墙角数枝梅，
凌寒独自开。
遥知不是雪，
为有暗香来。

THE PLUM BLOSSOM

There are a few sprays of plum blossoms in the corner. They are blooming alone in the cold wind. Why do I know they are not snow though viewing from a distance? That's because of the secret fragrance they send out.

Notes

1 王安石
Wang Anshi (1021-1086), whose courtesy name was Jiefu and pseudonym was Banshan, was an eminent statesman, thinker and literary man in the Northern Song Dynasty, ranking among the eight great men of letters in the Tang and Song dynasties. His poems focus on making arguments in a powerful style.

2 凌寒
to brave bitter cold

3 暗香
the pleasant fragrance of the plum blossoms

Famous quote

○ 遥知不是雪，为有暗香来。
These two lines reveal the plum blossom's daring and noble spirit against the severe cold. The plum blossom is as pure as snow and even better than snow because of its fragrance, implying the great charm of people who are strong and noble.

山水画二
Painting No.2

2 寻隐者不遇

唐·贾岛

松下问童子,
言师采药去。
只在此山中,
云深不知处。

SEARCHING FOR THE HERMIT IN VAIN

I asked a young lad under a pine tree in the mountain about his master's whereabouts and was told that he had gone to gather medicinal herbs. The hermit must have been somewhere in the mountain, but his young disciple had no idea about where exactly he was because of the thick mist.

Notes

1 贾岛

Jia Dao (779-843), whose courtesy name was Langxian, was a poet in the Tang Dynasty who worked hard on the exquisiteness of his works. Most of his poems depict natural sceneries and leisurely feelings in a simple and unsophisticated way.

2 隐者

In ancient times, it referred to a person who would rather live as a hermit in mountains than take up an official post. "者" means a certain kind of person.

Famous quote

松下问童子,言师采药去。
只在此山中,云深不知处。

These four lines imply several questions made by the visitor, showing the visitor's sincerity. The whole event, though complicated, is depicted in a concise and simple style. The pine in the poem signifies the hermit's upright character and the clouds stand for his noble spirit. The poem shows that the visitor admires the hermit more after failing in meeting him.

山水画 三
Painting No.3

3 登鹳雀楼

唐·王之涣

白日依山尽，
黄河入海流。
○ 欲穷千里目，
更上一层楼。

ASCENDING THE STORK TOWER

The bright sun fades away along the mountain, and the Yellow River flows into the vast sea. Now you have to climb one storey higher for a further and broader view.

Notes

1 王之涣

Wang Zhihuan (688-742), whose courtesy name was Jiling, was a poet in the flourishing period of the Tang Dynasty who was famous for his bold and passionate poems about the frontier landscape.

2 鹳雀楼

The Stork Tower, originally located in Yongji City, Shanxi Province, was a three-storeyed tower on which storks often perched, thus the name.

Famous quote

○ 欲穷千里目，更上一层楼。

These two lines embody the poet's striving spirit and great foresight and at the same time reveal the profound philosophic idea that "you can see far only when you stand high".

山水画 四
Painting No.4

4 鹿柴

唐·王维

空山不见人，
但闻人语响。
返景入深林，
复照青苔上。

AT THE LUZHAI HERMITAGE

In the deep silent mountain, I see nobody but hear some voices. The light of the setting sun penetrates into the dense forests, falls and shines on the green moss which is seldom exposed to the sun.

Notes

1 王维
Wang Wei (701-761), whose courtesy name was Mojie, was a poet in the Tang Dynasty good at writing about rural sceneries and landscapes. He knew a lot about Buddhism and was a versatile person famous for his poetry, calligraphy and painting.

2 鹿柴
Luzhai was the name of a scenery spot in Wangchuan, which was located in the present-day Lantian County, Shaanxi Province. It was the place where Wang Wei spent the later years of his life as a hermit.

3 返景
It refers to the reflected rays of the setting sun. "景" here means sunlight.

Famous quote

○ 返景入深林，复照青苔上。
These two lines compare the light of the setting sun with the darkness in the mountain forest, making the forest seem even deeper and quieter.

山水画 五
Painting No.5

5 独坐敬亭山

唐·李白

众鸟高飞尽,
孤云独去闲。
○ 相看两不厌,
只有敬亭山。

SITTING ALONE AT MOUNT JINGTING

All the birds fly away from the mountain. The last cloud in the sky, unwilling to stay around, drifts away at leisure. Nothing but Jingting Mountain stays here with me. We stare at each other without loathing each other. Who can understand my feelings better than the high Jingting Mountain?

Notes

1 李白

Li Bai (701-762), also called Taibai by his courtesy name, styled himself Qinglian Jushi or Immortal in Exile. As the greatest romantic poet in the Tang Dynasty, he was acknowledged as the "Poet Immortal". His poems, mostly about landscapes and the poet's inner feelings, are full of vigor, force and imagination.

2 敬亭山

Jingting Mountain is located in the northern part of Xuanzhou City, Anhui Province.

Famous quote

○ 相看两不厌,只有敬亭山。

These two lines reveal the poet's love for Jingting Mountain by means of personification. The poet and the mountain stare at each other in silence and their affectionate feelings are highlighted by the silence.

山水画 六
Painting No.6

6 乐游原

唐 · 李商隐

向晚意不适,
驱车登古原。
夕阳无限好,
只是近黄昏。

THE HAPPY UPLANDS

Towards evening, I feel out of spirits, so I mount to the old uplands on my cart to enjoy the sunset and relieve my boredom. The setting sun is extremely gorgeous; only the dusk is approaching.

Notes

1. **李商隐**
   Li Shangyin (813–858), whose courtesy name was Yishan and pseudonym was Yuxisheng, was a famous poet in the late Tang Dynasty. His poems are well-known for innovative ideas, gorgeous styles and deep feelings.

2. **乐游原**
   Leyouyuan, or the Happy Uplands, located in the south of Chang'an (present-day Xi'an), was then the highest point in Chang'an City.

3. **向晚意不适**
   This line means that the poet was in a bad mood when the evening came.
   向晚: dusk; **意**: feeling, mood; **不适**: bad, unhappy.

4. **古原**
   Guyuan, literally the old uplands, refers to Leyouyuan, which has been a tourist attraction since the Western Han Dynasty.

Famous quote

○ 夕阳无限好,只是近黄昏。
On the surface, these two lines talk about the setting sun at dusk, but actually, they reveal the poet's deep anxiety over the ever passing time and the dream increasingly hard to be fulfilled.

山水画 七
Painting No.7

7 逢雪宿芙蓉山主人

唐·刘长卿

日暮苍山远，
天寒白屋贫。
○ 柴门闻犬吠，
风雪夜归人。

LODGING IN THE HIBISCUS MOUNTAIN ON A SNOWY NIGHT

Towards evening, I'm held up in a mountain. The rolling mountains appear to be far-reaching in the shades, and the cold weather makes the hut I'm lodging in seem even more dilapidated. At midnight, I'm suddenly woken up by a barking dog. It turns out that the host has returned home from the blizzard.

Notes

1 刘长卿
Liu Changqing (709-786), whose courtesy name was Wenfang, was a famous poet in the Tang Dynasty. His poems mostly talk about his unfulfilled political ambitions. He was good at depicting natural sceneries and his writing style was implicit, gentle, elegant and concise.

2 白屋
unpainted roughly built hut inhabited by the poor

<u>Famous quote</u>

○ 柴门闻犬吠，风雪夜归人。
These two lines describe in the briefest words the scenes of a traveler lodging in a hut at dusk, a dog barking and the host returning at night, revealing a desolate and silent sense of feeling.

山水画 八
Painting No.8

8 江雪 (jiāng xuě)

唐·柳宗元 (táng liǔ zōng yuán)

千山鸟飞绝，(qiān shān niǎo fēi jué,)
万径人踪灭。(wàn jìng rén zōng miè.)
○ 孤舟蓑笠翁，(gū zhōu suō lì wēng,)
独钓寒江雪。(dú diào hán jiāng xuě.)

SNOW ON THE RIVER

Not a single bird is seen on the surrounding mountains and not a single person is seen on the paths. An old man wearing a straw rain cape and hat is alone fishing in the river on such a cold snowy day.

Notes

1 柳宗元
Liu Zongyuan (773-819), called Zihou or Liu Hedong, was a literary man, philosopher and thinker in the Tang Dynasty, ranking among the eight great men of letters in the Tang and Song dynasties. His poems are exquisitely designed, mostly dealing with depression, grief, nostalgia and friendship.

2 江雪
This poem was written after the poet was demoted to a position in Yongzhou. Writing about the old man alone fishing in the river, the poet showed his own feelings of loneliness and depression.

3 绝
to vanish, to be extinct

4 万径
thousands of ways and paths

Famous quote

○ 孤舟蓑笠翁，独钓寒江雪。
These two lines depict in a detailed and meticulous way the image of an old man fishing alone in the river against a pure and silent background. The fishing man is aloof and proud, just like the poet himself. Though the poet finds himself in a lonely situation, he still keeps an unyielding and lofty mental state.

山水画 九
Painting No.9

9 宿建德江

唐·孟浩然

移舟泊烟渚，
日暮客愁新。
○ 野旷天低树，
江清月近人。

NIGHT SPENT ON THE JIANDE RIVER

The boat is moved to moor at the misty islet, and the twilight inspires sorrow in the heart of a person traveling far away from home. In the vast wilds, the sky in the distance seems lower than the trees; on the clear river, the reflection brings the moon closer to us.

Notes

1 孟浩然
Meng Haoran (689-740), commonly referred to as "Meng Xiangyang", was a renowned poet in the Tang Dynasty. His poems are mostly about pastoral landscapes.

2 建德江
Jiande River is the part of Xin'an River in Jiande City, Zhejiang Province.

3 烟渚
mist-shrouded small island

<u>Famous quote</u>

○ 野旷天低树，江清月近人。
These two lines express the poet's nostalgic feeling. In the vast and quiet world, the poet only has the moon by his side. The feeling is integrated into the scene, creating a lightly flavored and subtly implied sense of beauty.

山水画 十
Painting No.10

10 登幽州台歌

唐·陈子昂

前不见古人，
后不见来者。
念天地之悠悠，
独怆然而涕下。

ON THE TOP OF YOUZHOU TOWER

I see neither the wise king who once hired talents here nor a talent-hunting ruler in the future. I fall into tears as I think of the vast universe and the short life.

Notes

1 陈子昂
Chen Zi Ang (661-702), whose courtesy name was Boyu, was an innovative pioneer in the Tang poetry. His poems focus on expressing inner feelings and hope.

2 幽州台
Youzhou Tower, also called Yan Tower, was said to be the Golden Tower built under the order of a ruler of Kingdom Yan during the Warring States Period for the purpose of recruiting talented people. It was located in the present-day Daxing District, Beijing.

Famous quote

○ 念天地之悠悠，独怆然而涕下。
With the vast universe and the historical vicissitudes as background, these two lines reveal the poet's lament over his unfulfilled ambition to serve his country and fellow people.

山水画 十一
Painting No.11

11 咏柳

yǒng liǔ

唐·贺知章
táng hè zhī zhāng

碧玉妆成一树高，
bì yù zhuāng chéng yí shù gāo,

万条垂下绿丝绦。
wàn tiáo chuí xià lǜ sī tāo.

○ 不知细叶谁裁出，
bù zhī xì yè shuí cái chū,

二月春风似剪刀。
èr yuè chūn fēng sì jiǎn dāo.

ODE TO THE WILLOW

The high willow tree looks like a young lady decked out in jade green, and the thousands of twigs are the green ribbons on her dress. Who has cut out the slender leaves? No wonder the answer is the early spring wind, which is as sharp as a pair of scissors.

Notes

1 贺知章
He Zhizhang (659-744), whose courtesy name was Jizhen and pseudonym was Shichuang, was a poet and calligrapher in the Tang Dynasty. His poems are fresh, simple and sensitive.

2 咏
to describe an object by means of poetry, etc.

3 碧玉
green jade, used here as a metaphor for willow leaves in the spring.

Famous quote

○ 不知细叶谁裁出，二月春风似剪刀。
These two lines adopt a question-and-answer method to describe the slender willow leaves and extol the extremely creative spring.

山水画 十二

Painting No.12

12 清明

唐·杜牧

清明时节雨纷纷，
路上行人欲断魂。
借问酒家何处有？
牧童遥指杏花村。

ON THE QINGMING DAY

On the Qingming Day, the continuous drizzle is falling, and all the pedestrians are in a bad and gloomy mood. I want to have a drink so that I can stay warm and forget about the loneliness and sorrow. When I ask a cowboy where I can find a wine shop, he points at the village behind the beautiful apricot trees in the distance.

Notes

1 杜牧
Du Mu (803-852), whose courtesy name was Muzhi, was a renowned poet during the later years of the Tang Dynasty. His poems are characterized by beautiful words and bright images.

2 清明
Qingming is one of the 24 solar terms in the Chinese lunar calendar. It falls around April 5th in the Gregorian calendar. People take an outing or go tomb sweeping on this day.

3 欲断魂
to feel gloomy and sorrowful

<u>Famous quote</u>

清明时节雨纷纷，路上行人欲断魂。
This is a typical example of the integration of sceneries and feelings in classical Chinese poems. The drizzling rain adds to the gloomy mood of the pedestrians.

山水画 十三
Painting No.13

13 九月九日忆山东兄弟

唐·王维

独在异乡为异客，
每逢佳节倍思亲。
遥知兄弟登高处，
遍插茱萸少一人。

THINKING OF MY BROTHERS AT HOME ON THE DOUBLE NINTH FESTIVAL

As a wanderer traveling alone in a strange place, I miss my relative folks a lot, especially on festive occasions. I think of my brothers at home. When they climb up a mountain today, wearing dogwood sprays, they must be keenly aware of my absence and miss me from afar.

Notes

1 九月九日忆山东兄弟
The ninth day of the ninth lunar month is the Double Ninth Festival in China. Customs on this day include climbing mountains and drinking chrysanthemum wine.
忆: to miss, to think of;
山东: Puzhou, the hometown of the poet, located to the east of Mount Hua.

2 茱萸
The dogwood is a kind of fragrant plant Chinese people used to wear when they climbed mountains on the Double Ninth Festival in the belief that it could drive away evils.

Famous quote

独在异乡为异客，每逢佳节倍思亲。
It's only natural for a person who travels far away from home to miss his hometown and family, especially on festivals when family members are supposed to gather together. These two lines are often quoted as they reveal a sentiment shared by all humankind.

山水画 十四
Painting No.14

14 望庐山瀑布
wàng lú shān pù bù

唐·李白
táng · lǐ bái

日照香炉生紫烟，
rì zhào xiāng lú shēng zǐ yān,

遥看瀑布挂前川。
yáo kàn pù bù guà qián chuān.

飞流直下三千尺，
fēi liú zhí xià sān qiān chǐ,

疑是银河落九天。
yí shì yín hé luò jiǔ tiān.

A VIEW OF THE WATERFALL AT LUSHAN MOUNTAIN

When rays of sunshine fall on the Incense Burner Peak, water begins to evaporate, forming a purple haze. Viewing from afar, I see a white waterfall rushing down the high mountain as if the Milky Way is falling from the heaven.

Notes

1. 庐山
Lushan Mountain is a famous mountain located in Jiujiang City, Jiangxi Province. It has been a tourist resort since ancient times.

2. 香炉
The Incense Burner Peak in the northeastern part of Lushan Mountain is so named because it is shaped like an incense burner shrouded in the mist.

3. 三千尺
"三千尺" equals to one kilometer. Here, it is an exaggerative way to say that the mountain is very high.

4. 九天
It was believed by ancient Chinese people that the heaven had nine layers. "九天" was the ninth and highest layer. Here it refers to the heaven high above.

Famous quote

飞流直下三千尺，疑是银河落九天。
With such rhetorical means as exaggeration and metaphor as well as romantic imagination, these two lines depict the magnificent scene of the waterfall pouring down the mountain top. The vivid comparison between the waterfall and the Milky Way is a typical example of the poet's romantic and imaginative writing style.

山水画 十五
Painting No.15

15 黄鹤楼送孟浩然之广陵

唐 · 李白

故人西辞黄鹤楼，
烟花三月下扬州。
○ 孤帆远影碧空尽，
唯见长江天际流。

SEEING MENG HAORAN OFF TO GUANGLING AT THE YELLOW CRANE TOWER

It is in the late spring when my old friend Meng Haoran departs from the Yellow Crane Tower to the eastern city Yangzhou. Amid the glorious willows and flowers of March, his boat sets out alone and fades into the distant horizon. Now I can see nothing but the ever flowing Yangtze River.

Notes

1 黄鹤楼
The Yellow Crane Tower is located to the south of the Yangtze River in Wuhan City, Hubei Province.

2 之广陵
It means "to leave for Guangling".
之: to go to, to leave for;
广陵: present-day Yangzhou City, Jiangsu Province.

3 故人
old friend, here referring to Meng Haoran

<u>Famous quote</u>

○ 孤帆远影碧空尽，唯见长江天际流。
In these two lines, the poet's affection towards his friend is shown through the depiction of sceneries. Although the friend has gone away, the poet still stares at the billowy river as if it can bring all his good wishes to his friend.

山水画 十六
Painting No.16

16 早发白帝城

táng · lǐ bái
唐 · 李白

zhāo cí bái dì cǎi yún jiān,
朝 辞 白 帝 彩 云 间,
qiān lǐ jiāng líng yí rì huán.
千 里 江 陵 一 日 还。
liǎng àn yuán shēng tí bú zhù,
○ 两 岸 猿 声 啼 不 住,
qīng zhōu yǐ guò wàn chóng shān.
轻 舟 已 过 万 重 山。

DEPARTURE AT MORN FROM BAIDI TOWN

I depart from the mist-shrouded Baidi Town in the morning. It takes me only one day to reach Jiangling, which is several hundred kilometers away. Amid the ceaseless chatter of monkeys on both banks, my light boat has already left rows of mountains behind it.

Notes

1 早发白帝城
早发: to depart in the morning. Baidi Town is located on Baidi Mountain in the eastern part of present-day Fengjie County, Chongqing. In the year of 759, Li Bai was on his way to exile in Yelang (an ancient county) when the punishment imposed on him was remitted. Baidi Town was where he set out on his journey back to Jiangling.

2 彩云间
Baidi Town, high in elevation, was often shrouded in mists, which appeared colorful under the sunshine. As a result, the whole town seemed as if surrounded by rosy clouds.

3 江陵
Jiangling, present-day Jingzhou City, Hubei Province, was about 1200 li (equal to 600 kilometers) away from Baidi Town.

4 万重山
rows of mountains

Famous quote

○ 两岸猿声啼不住,轻舟已过万重山。
These two lines use the echo of the undulating monkey sounds to set off the scene of a light boat speeding forward. Sailing the boat, the poet feels carefree and excited. After a long spell of hardship, the poet finally finds back his passion, ambition and pleasure.

山水画 十七
Painting No.17

17 绝句 (jué jù)

唐 · 杜甫 (táng · dù fǔ)

两个黄鹂鸣翠柳，
(liǎng gè huáng lí míng cuì liǔ)
一行白鹭上青天。
(yì háng bái lù shàng qīng tiān)
窗含西岭千秋雪，
(chuāng hán xī lǐng qiān qiū xuě)
门泊东吴万里船。
(mén bó dōng wú wàn lǐ chuán)

A QUATRAIN

Two yellow orioles are warbling in a green willow when a file of white egrets flies high into the azure sky. Looking out of the window, I see the perpetual snow on Minshan Mountain in the west and a boat anchored by my door which is bound for the eastern coast thousands of miles away.

Notes

1 杜甫
Du Fu (712-770), whose courtesy name was Zimei, was the greatest realistic poet in the Tang Dynasty. Equally popular as Li Bai, he was acknowledged as the "Poet Sage". His poems, mostly dealing with the political events and social life at his time, are commonly referred to as the "poems of history", which are deep and depressed in style.

2 东吴
Eastern Wu refers to the southeastern coastal area in the lower reaches of the Yangtze River. It belonged to Kingdom Wu in the ancient times and was located in the east of Wu.

Famous quote

○ 两个黄鹂鸣翠柳，一行白鹭上青天。
The first line describes the scenery nearby, while the second depicts the scenery faraway. The images, with varied colors, form a lively and bright picture, revealing the pleasant mood of the poet.

山水画 十八
Painting No.18

18 题西林壁

宋·苏轼

横看成岭侧成峰,
远近高低各不同。
不识庐山真面目,
只缘身在此山中。

WRITTEN ON THE WALL OF XILIN TEMPLE

When I look at Lushan Mountain, I see ridges when viewing from one side and peaks when viewing from another. The views of the mountain, far and near, high and low, vary widely. I cannot tell the true looks of Lushan Mountain, because I myself am in the mountain.

Notes

1 苏轼
Su Shi (1037-1101), whose courtesy name was Zizhan and pseudonym was Dongpo Jushi, was a famous literary man, calligrapher and painter in the Northern Song Dynasty. He was one of the eight great men of letters in the Tang and Song dynasties. His poems and prose works are bold in style and rich in imagination.

2 题西林壁
The title indicates the poem was written on the wall of Xilin Temple, a temple located on Lushan Mountain.
题: to write.

3 真面目
true face, here referring to the full view of Lushan Mountain

Famous quote

○ 不识庐山真面目,只缘身在此山中。
These two lines are profoundly philosophic. In order to get a full and correct view of a subject, one has to study every aspect of it in an objective way rather than confining oneself to the small circle of the subject.

山水画 十九
Painting No.19

19 饮湖上，初晴后雨

宋·苏轼

水光潋滟晴方好，
山色空濛雨亦奇。
欲把西湖比西子，
淡妆浓抹总相宜。

DRINKING ON THE WEST LAKE, ENJOYING THE RAIN AFTER THE SUNSHINE

When the weather is sunny, the water in the West Lake ripples and sparkles under the rays of sunlight; when it is overcast or rainy, the West Lake shows another kind of beauty amid the faintly discernible and mist-shrouded mountains. Just like the beautiful lady Xizi, the West Lake is beautiful and gorgeous no matter it is richly adorned or plainly dressed.

Notes

1 饮湖上
to drink wine on the West Lake in Hangzhou

2 潋滟
(of the water) rippling and sparkling

3 西子
Xizi is another name for Xi Shi, who was a beautiful girl in Kingdom Yue during the Spring and Autumn Period. She was one of the four great beauties in ancient China, the other three being Wang Zhaojun, Diao Chan and Yang Yuhuan.

Famous quote

○ 欲把西湖比西子，淡妆浓抹总相宜。
People today often quote these two lines to extol the beauty of the West Lake. Both the West Lake and Xizi are beautiful in a graceful, and more importantly, natural way. By comparing the West Lake to the beautiful lady Xizi, the poem gives life to the lake and captures its very essence in a unique manner.

山水画 二十
Painting No.20

20 登飞来峰

宋 · 王安石

飞来山上千寻塔,
闻说鸡鸣见日升。
不畏浮云遮望眼,
自缘身在最高层。

ASCENDING FEILAI PEAK

There is a towering pagoda at the summit of Feilai Peak. It is said that standing in the pagoda, one can see the rise of the sun at the crow of the rooster. I am not afraid that the floating clouds blot out my commanding view, because I'm already standing on the top floor of the pagoda.

Notes

1. 飞来峰
Feilai Peak, also called Lingjiu Peak, stands right in front of the Lingyin Temple in Hangzhou, Zhejiang Province. There was a pagoda called Yingtian on it during the Tang and Song dynasties, so it is commonly referred to as the "Tower Mountain".

2. 千寻塔
In ancient times, one xun equals 8/3 meters. A pagoda with a height of 1,000 xun is a very high one.

3. 浮云
floating clouds, used here as a metaphor for treacherous people

Famous quote

○ 不畏浮云遮望眼,自缘身在最高层。
These two lines reveal the poet's lofty and far-sighted spirit as well as his determination to overcome difficulties. Moreover, they give vivid expression to the philosophic idea that "you can see far only when you stand high".

山水画 二十一
Painting No.21

21 秋词

唐·刘禹锡

自古逢秋悲寂寥，
我言秋日胜春朝。
晴空一鹤排云上，
便引诗情到碧霄。

AUTUMN SONG

Through the ages, people always sigh over autumn, believing it to be somber and desolate. In my eyes, however, autumn days are even more vigorous than the bright spring. Look! In the clear sky, a crane flies into the clouds, and my poetic verve is aroused and soars to the blue sky.

Notes

1 刘禹锡
Liu Yuxi (772-842), whose courtesy name was Mengde, was a renowned poet during the middle and later years of the Tang Dynasty. His poetic style being vigorous and fresh, he was acknowledged as the "Poetic Giant".

2 悲寂寥
悲: sad, sorrowful; 寂寥: lonely, miserable.

3 排云上
排云上: to soar into the sky; 排: to push, to strike.

Famous quote

自古逢秋悲寂寥，我言秋日胜春朝。
Different from other Chinese verses about autumn, these two lines extol the beauty and splendor of autumn in an inspirational way rather than lamenting over it. Embodied in the lines is the positive and striving spirit of the poet.

山水画 二十二
Painting No.22

22 滁州西涧

唐 · 韦应物

独怜幽草涧边生，
上有黄鹂深树鸣。
春潮带雨晚来急，
野渡无人舟自横。

THE WEST RAVINE IN CHUZHOU

I like the grass grown by the ravine side a lot. When it grows quietly and vigorously on the bank, orioles are chirping pleasantly deep in the trees. The river rises and its speed quickens because of the spring rain in the evening. In the twilight, nobody is seen at the deserted ferry, except for a small boat lying there alone.

Notes

1. **韦应物**
   Wei Yingwu (737– around 792), was a poet of the Tang Dynasty who was good at writing about pastoral landscapes in a quiet and natural way.

2. **滁州西涧**
   滁州: present-day Chuzhou City, Anhui Province;
   西涧: a small stream in the western suburbs of Chuzhou City.

3. **野渡**
   unsupervised ferry in a deserted place

Famous quote

- 春潮带雨晚来急，野渡无人舟自横。
  These two lines depict the scene of a sudden rain with a spring tide and a small boat lying alone on the water, revealing the poet's love for nature and leisurely life.

山水画 二十三
Painting No.23

23 游子吟

唐 · 孟郊

慈母手中线，
游子身上衣。
临行密密缝，
意恐迟迟归。
○ 谁言寸草心，
报得三春晖？

SONG OF A WANDERER

A fond-hearted mother, needle and thread in her hands, is making clothes for her boy who is about to travel far away from home. She sews carefully and mends thoroughly for fear that nobody would mend his clothes during the long journey. Who says the inch-long grass can repay the spring sunshine under which it grows?

Notes

1　孟郊
Meng Jiao (751–814), whose courtesy name was Dongye, was a poet of the Tang Dynasty. His poems are unsophisticated but profound, mostly talking about impoverished life.

2　游子吟
游子: person who travels or lives away from home;
吟: to sing softly.

3　寸草心
寸草: little grass, here metaphorically meaning one's child;
心: grass stem, also one's piety and gratitude towards his/her parents.

4　三春晖
三春晖: sunshine in the spring, standing for mother love;
三春: the three months or periods in the spring, i.e. early spring, mid-spring and late spring.

<u>Famous quote</u>

○ 谁言寸草心，报得三春晖？
By such rhetorical means as vivid metaphor and comparison, the two lines reveal the son's deep gratitude towards his mother and his belief that one can never repay his/her mother's love just like the feeble grass can never repay the sunshine.

山水画 二十四
Painting No.24

24 山居秋暝

唐 · 王维

空山新雨后，
天气晚来秋。
明月松间照，
清泉石上流。
竹喧归浣女，
莲动下渔舟。
随意春芳歇，
王孙自可留。

AN AUTUMN EVENING IN THE MOUNTAINS

The mountain becomes clearer after a fresh rain and the weather colder on the autumn evening. The moon quietly sheds its beams through the forest of pine trees, and the jingling spring streams over the rocks. Whispers and giggles are heard from the bamboo groves as the washer girls are on their way home; the lotus leaves sway as a fishing boat is set afloat on the water. Let the fragrant spring fade with time. When autumn comes, the wanderer can also have a good time in the mountain.

Notes

1 暝
sunset, dusk

2 王孙
hermit, also the poet himself

Famous quote

○ 明月松间照，清泉石上流。
These two lines depict the fresh, quiet and serene scenery in the mountain after a rain. The whole picture is naturally appealing and serenely beautiful.

山水画 二十五
Painting No.25

25 赋得古原草送别

唐·白居易

离离原上草，
一岁一枯荣。
○ 野火烧不尽，
春风吹又生。
远芳侵古道，
晴翠接荒城。
又送王孙去，
萋萋满别情。

GRASS ON THE ANCIENT PLAIN — FAREWELL TO A FRIEND

The green grass spreads upon the ancient plain. It dies and flourishes each year from fall to spring. Even fire cannot burn it up, because it will surge back when vernal breezes blow. Its fresh fragrance overruns the ancient road, and its greenness meets with the ruined town in the sun. When I see my close friend off once again, the green grass seems to be filled with the parting feeling as well.

Notes

1. 白居易
   Bai Juyi (772-846), whose courtesy name was Letian and pseudonym was Xiangshan Jushi, was an eminent realistic poet in the Tang Dynasty. He is regarded as one of the top three poets in the Tang Dynasty, the other two being Li Bai and Du Fu. His poems use plain and easy words to reveal the thoughts and wishes of lower-class people.

2. 王孙
   nobleman, here referring to the friend of the poet

Famous quote

○ 野火烧不尽，春风吹又生。
With three pairs of antithetical words, i.e. "野火/春风", "烧/吹" and "尽/生", these two lines concisely and vividly extol the indomitable vitality of newly emerging things.

山水画 二十六
Painting No.26

26 送杜少府之任蜀州

唐 · 王勃

城阙辅三秦,
风烟望五津。
与君离别意,
同是宦游人。
○ 海内存知己,
天涯若比邻。
无为在歧路,
儿女共沾巾。

FAREWELL TO PREFECT DU ON HIS WAY TO SHUZHOU

The Three-Qin area guards the city of Chang'an. Looking far into the distance, I can faintly see the five ferry terminals amid the wind and mist. I am loath to part with you because we are both officials in a strange land. Remote distance cannot obstruct our close relation, as we are intimate friends wherever we are. When we part at crossroads, it's not necessary for us to wet our front garments with too many emotional tears as the sentimental saplings do.

Notes

1. 王勃
   Wang Bo (649-676), whose courtesy name was Zi'an, was an eminent poet in the Tang Dynasty who died at an early age. His poems depict his personal life in an unsophisticated and fresh manner.

2. 送杜少府之任蜀州
   少府: an official title;
   之: to go, to leave for;
   蜀州: present-day Chongzhou City, Sichuan Province.

3. 三秦
   三秦, literally "Three Qin", was a general term for the area near Chang'an City, Shaanxi Province. It was originally part of the ancient Kingdom Qin. After Qin perished, Xiang Yu divided this area into three parts, thus the name.

4. 歧路
   歧路: crossroads. Ancient Chinese people used to part with each other at crossroads.

Famous quote

○ 海内存知己,天涯若比邻。
These two lines talk about the deep affection between friends. True friendship won't be impeded by time or distance. The attitude embodied here is positive and open-minded.

山水画 二十七
Painting No.27

27 无题

唐·李商隐

相见时难别亦难，
东风无力百花残。
春蚕到死丝方尽，
蜡炬成灰泪始干。
晓镜但愁云鬓改，
夜吟应觉月光寒。
蓬山此去无多路，
青鸟殷勤为探看。

NO TITLE

It is hard to meet you, even harder to part with you. The scene of the late spring when the east wind becomes languid and hundreds of flowers wither only adds to my sadness. The spring silkworms won't stop producing silk until death and the tear-like wax won't stop dripping until the candle is burnt out. When I make myself up in the morning, I look into the mirror and fear that one day my thick hair would turn grey and my looks would be gone. When I'm singing at night, I keenly feel the chill of the moon. The person I miss is living in a place as far away as the island in ancient mythology. How much I wish that I had a messenger like Blue Bird to send my messages to my lover!

Notes

1 丝方尽
"丝" (silk) sounds the same as "思" (to miss sb.) in Chinese. "丝方尽" means one wouldn't stop missing his/her lover until death.

2 云鬓
thick and gorgeous hair of a young lady, here used as a metaphor for youth

3 蓬山
Peng Mountain, or Penglai Mountain, is a legendary mountain island, which here stands for the place where the person one is missing lives.

4 青鸟
The Blue Bird is a messenger-bird for the mother-goddess in ancient mythology.

Famous quote

春蚕到死丝方尽，蜡炬成灰泪始干。
These two lines express one's longing for the beloved one, revealing not only sorrow and pain, but also a lingering persistence and burning desire. This quote, originally a portrayal of true love and unswerving loyalty, is now often used as a metaphor for teachers' selfless dedication to their students.

山水画 二十八
Painting No.28

28 明日歌

明·文嘉

明日复明日，
明日何其多！
我生待明日，
万事成蹉跎。
世人若被明日累，
春去秋来老将至。
朝看水东流，
暮看日西坠。
百年明日能几何？
请君听我明日歌。

SONG OF TOMORROW

There is one tomorrow after another. How many tomorrows there are! If we always wait until tomorrow to do something, we'll miss all the opportunities in our lives. If people are cumbered by tomorrow, time will make them old before they know. They see the river flowing eastward in the morning and the sun setting in the west at dusk. How many tomorrows can we have? Please listen to my song of tomorrow.

Notes

1 文嘉
Wen Jia (1501-1583), whose courtesy name was Xiucheng and pseudonym was Wenshui, was the second son of the famous calligrapher and painter Wen Zhengming in the Ming Dynasty. Wen Jia was good at poetry, calligraphy and painting.

2 蹉跎
to idle one's time away

Famous quote

明日复明日，明日何其多！
我生待明日，万事成蹉跎。
These lines warn people against wasting time and advise them to do things today rather than waiting till tomorrow. We can get many things back through efforts, but for time, we can do nothing to make it stay.

山水画 二十九
Painting No.29

29 水调歌头
shuǐ diào gē tóu

宋·苏轼
sòng sū shì

明月几时有?
míng yuè jǐ shí yǒu?

把酒问青天。
bǎ jiǔ wèn qīng tiān.

不知天上宫阙,
bù zhī tiān shàng gōng què,

今夕是何年?
jīn xī shì hé nián?

我欲乘风归去,
wǒ yù chéng fēng guī qù,

又恐琼楼玉宇,
yòu kǒng qióng lóu yù yǔ,

高处不胜寒。
gāo chù bù shèng hán.

起舞弄清影,
qǐ wǔ nòng qīng yǐng,

何似在人间?
hé sì zài rén jiān?

转朱阁,
zhuǎn zhū gé,

低绮户,
dī qǐ hù,

照无眠。
zhào wú mián.

不应有恨,
bù yīng yǒu hèn,

何事长向别时圆?
hé shì cháng xiàng bié shí yuán?

人有悲欢离合,
rén yǒu bēi huān lí hé,

月有阴晴圆缺,
yuè yǒu yīn qíng yuán quē,

此事古难全。
cǐ shì gǔ nán quán.

○ 但愿人长久,
dàn yuàn rén cháng jiǔ,

千里共婵娟。
qiān lǐ gòng chán juān.

WHEN DID THE MOON BECOME CLEAR AND BRIGHT

When did the moon become clear and bright? I ask the blue sky, a cup of wine in my hand. I don't know what year or what day it is in heaven where immortals live. I'd like to fly back to heaven with the wind, yet I fear the crystal and jade mansions are much too high and cold for me. With all these thoughts, I dance under the moon with my moon lit shadow. It seems as if I'm dancing in heaven amid the clouds rather than in the human world.

The moon comes around the red mansion and hangs low outside the window. It shines upon the sleepless one. Bearing no grudge against people, why does it tend to be full when people are apart? People have sorrows or joys, and they part or meet again. The moon may be bright or dim, and she may wax or wane. These rules have been going on since the beginning of time. May the people I love be blessed with longevity! Though far apart, we are still able to share the beauty of the moon together.

Notes

1 水调歌头
"水调歌头" is the name of a tune. In ancient China, ci poems were composed to tunes for singing. The poet wrote this poem on a mid-autumn evening when the moon was full and bright.

2 今夕是何年
今夕是何年: what year is it. According to ancient mythology, for three days in heaven, a thousand years have already passed on earth. Ancient people believed that the immortals and mortals had different sys-tems of time. That was why the poet asked this question.

3 乘风归去
乘风归去: to go back to heaven with the wind. The poet here romantically considered himself as an immortal from heaven.

Famous quote

○ 但愿人长久,千里共婵娟。
These two lines mean that the common love for the bright moon conquers the limits of time and space and brings people who are thousands of miles away together.

山水画 三十
Painting No.30

30 虞美人

南唐·李煜

春花秋月何时了？
往事知多少？
小楼昨夜又东风，
故国不堪回首月明中。
雕阑玉砌应犹在，
只是朱颜改。
○ 问君能有几多愁，
恰似一江春水向东流。

TO THE TUNE OF "FAIR LADY YU"

When did the moonlit autumn and the flowery spring come to the end? How many memories of the past time do I have? The vernal wind stroked my attic again last night, yet I could not bear to look back at the lost land under the moonlight.

The carved balustrades and marble steps may be the same as they were before, but those tender and beautiful faces have already changed a lot. If you ask how sad I am, my sorrow is just like the overbrimming river flowing east in spring.

Notes

1 李煜
Li Yu (937-978), originally named Congjia and called Chongguang by his courtesy name, was the last lord of the Southern Tang Dynasty. He had been on the throne for 15 years before surrendering to the Song Regime. This ci poem reveals the poet's deep longing for his homeland.

2 虞美人
"Fair Lady Yu" was a tune coming from the imperial music office of the Tang Dynasty. It was originally composed to extol Xiang Yu's favorite concubine Lady Yu.

3 春花秋月
It is short for "the blooming flowers in spring and the full moon in mid-autumn", symbolizing the best time in one's life.

4 小楼
It refers to the building in which the poet lived after being captured by the Song Regime and detained in Bianjing (present-day Kaifeng, Henan Province).

5 故国
It refers to Jinling (present-day Nanjing), the capital of the Southern Tang Dynasty.

Famous quote

○ 问君能有几多愁，恰似一江春水向东流。
With an appealing metaphor, these two lines emphasize the depth and infinity of sorrow. The sorrow is compared to the billowy water which is forever flowing eastwards, no matter in the day or at night. It feels like sorrows of all ages are embodied in these two lines.

画家简历
Curriculum Vitae

袁丽莉

1956	出生于上海市，1992年起旅居德国
1977-81	复旦大学日本文学专业毕业
1989-90	日本大坂市立大学文学部比较教育专业进修
1994-97	德国波鸿鲁尔大学艺术史专业学习
1999	北京中央美院中日专家执教重彩画高级研修班

近年来重要的个人展和集体参展

2000	卡喀市立博物馆，德国
2001	中央美院画廊重彩画获奖作品展，中国北京
2002	艺术家支助阿富汗慈善展，德国科隆
2006	妇女艺术馆艺术展，德国波恩
2007	杜伊斯堡文化与历史博物馆，德国
2008	第10届国际艺术展，德国欧斯那卜克
2008	第11届国际艺术展，瑞士萨尔茨堡
2011	柏林中国文化中心，德国

获奖情况

2001	首届中国重彩画大展优秀奖，中国美术家协会主办
2002	首届中国书画小精品创作大赛银奖，翰墨书画院等主办
2005	国际华人诗书画印艺术大展优秀奖，文化部中国画研究院主办
2008	入选全国第七届工笔画大展，中国工笔画家协会主办

出版成果

2010	出版画册《山水之旅——水墨画与古诗》雷谢特出版社（Reichert Verlag），德国威斯巴顿

Artist: Yuan Lili

1956	born in Shanghai, China
since 1992	living in Germany
1977-81	Fudan University, China BA in Japanese Literature
1989-90	Department of Literature, Osaka City University, Japan: Further study in Comparative Education
1994-97	Ruhr University Bochum, Germany: Further study in History of Art
1999	Central Academy of Fine Art, Beijing, China: Expert teaching in the advanced training class of heavy color painting

Major Individual and Collective Exhibitions in Recent Years

2000	Kalkar's City Museum, Germany
2001	Exhibition of Award-winning works of Color Painting in Central Academy of Fine Art, Beijing, China
2002	Charity Art Exhibition for Aiding Afghanistan, Cologne, Germany
2006	Art Exhibition in Women's Museum, Bonn, Germany
2007	Duisburg Museum of Culture and City History, Germany
2008	10th International Art Fair, Osnabrück, Germany
2008	11th International Art Fair, Salzburg, Switzerland
2011	Chinese Cultural Center in Berlin, Germany

Awards

2001	Award of Excellence in the First Art Show of Chinese Heavy Color Paintings Sponsor: Chinese Artists Association
2002	Silver Award in the First Creation Contest of Small Chinese Calligraphic and Painting Works Sponsor: Ink Painting and Calligraphy Institute, etc.
2005	Award of Excellence in the International Chinese Art Fair of Poetry, Calligraphy, Painting and Printing Sponsor: Academy of Chinese Painting under China's Ministry of Culture
2008	Exhibitor in the Seventh National Elaborate-Style Painting Show Sponsor: Chinese Elaborate-Style Painters Association

Publications

2010	"A Journey of Chinese Landscapes – Ink Paintings and Ancient Poems", an album of paintings published by Reichert Verlag, Wiesbaden, Germany

版本说明
Imprint

图书在版编目(CIP)数据

山水间: 读诗赏画学汉语 / 袁丽莉绘; 北京语言
大学对外汉语教材研发中心编写 —— 北京:
北京语言大学出版社, 2011.9
ISBN 978-7-5619-3145-5

Ⅰ.①山… Ⅱ.①袁… ②北… Ⅲ.①汉语 – 对外汉语教学
– 语言读物 Ⅳ.①H195.5

中国版本图书馆CIP数据核字(2011)第199921号

书　　名:	山水间——读诗赏画学汉语
策　　划:	张　健
责任编辑:	付彦白　孙玉婷
责任印制:	汪学发

出版发行: 北京语言大学出版社
社　　址: 北京市海淀区学院路15号　邮政编码: 100083
网　　址: www.blcup.com
电　　话: 国内发行 8610-82303650/3591/3651
　　　　　海外发行 8610-82300309/0361/3080/3365
　　　　　编辑部 8610-82303647/3592
　　　　　读者服务部 8610-82303653/3908
　　　　　网上订购电话 8610-82303668
　　　　　客户服务信箱 service@blcup.net
印　　刷: 北京联兴盛业印刷股份有限公司
经　　销: 全国新华书店
版　　次: 2011年12月第1版　2011年12月第1次印刷
开　　本: 889毫米×1194毫米　1/16　印张: 4.5
字　　数: 55千字
书　　号: ISBN 978-7-5619-3145-5/ H·11190
　　　　　06500

绘画: 袁丽莉, 德国
© All Paintings by Lili Yuan, Krefeld, Germany
www.chinaart-lili.de

书籍和封面设计: 吴祎萌 工作室, 德国柏林
Cover and book design by Yimeng Wu, Berlin
www.yimengwu.com

书中使用的拉丁语字体 Sung New Roman 取自于德国的字体设计师 Roman Wilhelm (罗小弟) 的设计。该字体的设计形成受中文宋体的影响, 两个不同字体系统的混合给人们一种和谐的整体形象。
The latin font "Sung New Roman" used in this book was designed by German typographer Roman Wilhelm (罗小弟). Its styles are related to the Chinese Song script; it enables a harmonious mixture between the two different writing systems.

凡有印装质量问题, 本社负责调换。电话: 8610-82303590
Printed in China.

光盘目录
CD Contents

1	梅花 ‖ 王安石	"The Plum Blossom" by Wang Anshi
2	寻隐者不遇 ‖ 贾岛	"Searching for the Hermit in Vain" by Jia Dao
3	登鹳雀楼 ‖ 王之涣	"Ascending the Stork Tower" by Wang Zhihuan
4	鹿柴 ‖ 王维	"At the Luzhai Hermitage" by Wang Wei
5	独坐敬亭山 ‖ 李白	"Sitting Alone at Mount Jingting" by Li Bai
6	乐游原 ‖ 李商隐	"The Happy Uplands" by Li Shangyin
7	逢雪宿芙蓉山主人 ‖ 刘长卿	"Lodging in the Hibiscus Mountain on a Snowy Night" by Liu Changqing
8	江雪 ‖ 柳宗元	"Snow on the River" by Liu Zongyuan
9	宿建德江 ‖ 孟浩然	"Night Spent on the Jiande River" by Meng Haoran
10	登幽州台歌 ‖ 陈子昂	"On the Top of Youzhou Tower" by Chen Zi'ang
11	咏柳 ‖ 贺知章	"Ode to the Willow" by He Zhizhang
12	清明 ‖ 杜牧	"On the Qingming Day" by Du Mu
13	九月九日忆山东兄弟 ‖ 王维	"Thinking of My Brothers at Home on the Double Ninth Festival" by Wang Wei
14	望庐山瀑布 ‖ 李白	"A View of the Waterfall at Lushan Mountain" by Li Bai
15	黄鹤楼送孟浩然之广陵 ‖ 李白	"Seeing Meng Haoran Off to Guangling at the Yellow Crane Tower" by Li Bai
16	早发白帝城 ‖ 李白	"Departure at Morn from Baidi Town" by Li Bai
17	绝句 ‖ 杜甫	"A Quatrain" by Du Fu
18	题西林壁 ‖ 苏轼	"Written on the Wall of Xilin Temple" by Su Shi
19	饮湖上，初晴后雨 ‖ 苏轼	"Drinking on the West Lake, Enjoying the Rain after the Sunshine" by Su Shi
20	登飞来峰 ‖ 王安石	"Ascending Feilai Peak" by Wang Anshi
21	秋词 ‖ 刘禹锡	"Autumn Song" by Liu Yuxi
22	滁州西涧 ‖ 韦应物	"The West Ravine in Chuzhou" by Wei Yingwu
23	游子吟 ‖ 孟郊	"Song of a Wanderer" by Meng Jiao
24	山居秋暝 ‖ 王维	"An Autumn Evening in the Mountains" by Wang Wei
25	赋得古原草送别 ‖ 白居易	"Grass on the Ancient Plain—Farewell to a Friend" by Bai Juyi
26	送杜少府之任蜀州 ‖ 王勃	"Farewell to Prefect Du on His Way to Shuzhou" by Wang Bo
27	无题 ‖ 李商隐	"No Title" by Li Shangyin
28	明日歌 ‖ 文嘉	"Song of Tomorrow" by Wen Jia
29	水调歌头（明月几时有）‖ 苏轼	"When Did the Moon Become Clear and Bright" by Su Shi
30	虞美人 ‖ 李煜	"To the Tune of 'Fair Lady Yu'" by Li Yu